ASH & INK

AF528522

THE STORYTELLER'S COMPANION

Woven Blade

Ash and Ink

Published by Woven Ink Press
First Edition, 2025

ISBN: 978-93-343-6686-0

Cover design by Woven Blade

For permissions, collaborations, and contact:
bladewoven@gmail.com

Introduction

This isn't just a book you read.
It's a book you enter.

A forge of stories. A sanctuary of sparks. A blank space that waits for your ink.

Every page you touch here is alive with creation—where characters rise from shadows, where forgotten worlds are rebuilt, and where even a single line you write can light up someone else's path.

But here's the magic:
Ash and Ink grows with every storyteller who dares to add their voice.

Shape your world. And when you're ready—**share your story**.

The most powerful entries will be chosen and published in the upcoming edition of this very book.
Yes, you could be part of the next chapter. Literally.

Because in the end, this book belongs not to the author...
...but to those brave enough to pick up the pen.

Meet your Companions

RAIF

Raif walks with silence like an old tale unfolding in shadows. With a long coat that smells faintly of old pages and wind-swept journeys, he carries ink—not just to write, but to preserve forgotten truths. Calm and observant, Raif speaks only when needed—but when he does, his words stay with you, like an echo in the mountains.

He believes every person holds a story that matters—and he's here to help you find yours.

"The ink remembers even what the world forgets."
– Raif

SAFINA

Safina's footsteps are lighter than smoke, but she sees farther than most. Where Raif holds the ink, Safina brings the flame—not to burn, but to ignite wonder, imagination, and courage. With a glint in her eyes, she'll nudge you toward questions you've never asked—and ideas that could change everything.

Safina is your compass when the path twists unexpectedly. She knows that sometimes, the ash from old fires makes the richest soil.

"Stories grow where courage is planted." – Safina

STORYTELLER'S PROFILE

Name: ________________________________

Pen Name (optional):

____

Age: ____________

Date of Entry: ______________________

<u>Current Mood:</u>

Brave Curious Thoughtful Mysterious Restless

<u>What kind of stories call to you?</u>

(Check all that feel right)

☐ Adventure

☐ Magic & Mystery

☐ Real-life with a twist

☐ Stories of sacrifice

☐ Future worlds

☐ Lost places & forgotten voices

✍️ Choose Your Role:

☐ **Inkbearer (Recorder of truth)**
☐ **Ashwalker (Wanderer between stories)**
☐ **Fireweaver (Builder of emotion & drama)**
☐ **Quiet Blade (Soft speaker, sharp thinker)**

🧳 Three things you carry on your journey:

1-

2-

3-

Contents

Woven Ink

Restless

Raindrops tapped steadily on the window, and the clouds thundered softly. Nayel stared outside, lost in his thoughts. Everything looked calm, but inside him, he felt restless, like a quiet unease he couldn't shake. He wasn't ungrateful. He wasn't Unhappy either, but He always felt restlessness inside.

To others, Nayel showed many sides of himself. Some saw a thoughtful observer, others a cheerful friend. But maybe no one knew the real him. Did he have different personalities? Maybe only he knew.

He cared for the people he called "close," but he never let them see his true feelings. He dipped his pen into dark ink and wrote on a pale yellow page in his leather notebook: "What do you really want? Why do you keep running away? Why...?" Each question felt heavy in his mind.

Morning arrived, and he headed to school -a course he had chosen but no longer enjoyed. The work still interested him, but it didn't excite him anymore. At break, he laughed with friends, though inside he felt disappointed with himself. One friend said, "We need to focus, Nayel. Time is short. We have to decide our future."

Nayel wanted to find one thing to love and pursue with passion, like everyone else. In his world, people respected those dedicated to a single goal.
But Nayel's interests jumped from one thing to another until he lost track of them all. It was easier to get distracted or escape than to face his confusion.

One afternoon, he went to the garden with his notebook. Under the green leaves, he looked for answers. As he sat, an old man with a gray-streaked beard appeared next to him.

"What's your Cause?" the man asked.

Nayel blinked. "Did you talk to me?"

"I spoke to the restless soul," the man said.

"There is no Cause," Nayel answered. "It is just lost soul- tired and restless."

The old man took the notebook and read:
"A child's pain turned into pearls falling from the mother's eyes, Corruption drove people to madness, Strange forces troubled a generation, 'Activism'- the forgotten thing, The rise of personality worship..."

He looked up and asked, "And you say you have no Cause?"

"I just know to complain," Nayel said quietly. "I'm one of those people."

"No," the old man replied. "This isn't complaining -it's reflecting. It's observing -clearly."

Nayel shook his head. "All I see are problems. I have no vision. I live in shadows."

"Problems push people away," the old man said, closing the notebook. "But they also call for solutions.
Maybe you are the solution."

Nayel laughed softly. "Me?"
He turned to ask more, but there was no one; the old man had gone. The garden was still. Nayel sat alone, holding his notebook.

~ Woven Blade

This story comes from personal journal entries of Woven Blade that have been shaped into a short narrative. It blends real reflections with creative storytelling to guide you through Nayel's inner journey.

So, my Inkweavers, let me ask you something...

- What was the actual cause of Nayel?
- Was that old man actually real?
- How can Nayel be the solution itself?

Here's a direct extract from the Journal of Woven Blade, It's in raw form.

You actually don't need to pressurize yourself to the extent that you lose the originality, sometimes, a small personal idea or message is enough for the short scenes.

SO, YOUR HANDS ARE SHIVERING WRITING THIS,...
AH! SAIF, HOW MANY FACES OF YOURS HAVE YOU SEEN?

YES, SOME OF THEM ARE BRIGHT,
BUT, SOME OF THEM,...
THEY ARE INDEED THE DARKEST THINGS YOU'VE SEEN.

NEVER, SAIF,... NEVER SUBMIT TO THEM.
THEY CANNOT BE KILLED,
BUT, THE BATTLE WILL CONTINUE
&, AS A SOLDIER YOU WILL KEEP FIGHTING.

BE GRATEFUL TO YOUR GOD THAT YOU ARE AWARE OF THEM,
I FEAR FOR THOSE WHO HAVE SUBMITTED TO THEM WITHOUT EVEN TRYING TO FACE THEM!

~ Woven Blade

Freedom Zone

Welcome to Freedom Zone

This is your space. Your world. Your voice.
No rules. No limits. Just your ideas flowing onto the page.
Start a story. Sketch a feeling. Build a truth.
We're not telling you what to write--
we're just making room for your fire to catch.

BE PART OF THE UPCOMING EDITION

Your words matter. Your stories can move hearts, change minds, and light up corners of the world you've never seen.

Submit Your Story by Sending it to Us!

bladewoven@gmail.com

Must be your original work.

Selected entries will be featured in the next book!

INK MAY FADE, BUT YOUR STORY CAN OUTLIVE CENTURIES. IT ONLY BEGINS WHEN YOU DECIDE TO SHARE IT

Write the door you wish existed, then walk through slowly.

A blank page is not empty; it's listening.

Make your character choose, then make them pay attention

Stories are questions that learned to breathe.

THE FORGE OF INK

The Forge of Ink

<u>Where your stories are not told, but forged.</u>

Welcome, storyteller. You've entered the heart of this book -a place where characters awaken, worlds take shape, and stories burn bright. This section helps you shape ideas that aren't just creative, but deeply meaningful.

Raif and Safina will guide you through three creative benches in this forge:

- <u>Character Forge</u>
- <u>Worldbuilder's Workshop</u>
- <u>Plot Lab</u>

Each station is hands-on. You don't need to get it perfect. You just need to begin. Scribble, doodle your thoughts, write wild and then refine. This is your forge -light it.

Character Forge

Build a character from the inside out.

True characters aren't built from looks. They're built from choices, scars, and sparks.

Activity 1: The Ghost

What painful moment still echoes in your character's heart?

This ghost doesn't have to be dramatic. Even quiet wounds shape powerful stories.

ACTIVITY 2: Want vs. Need

What does your character desperately want?

What truth must they learn or accept?

Sometimes, what we want isn't what we need.

Desire drives the plot. But need gives your story its heart.

ACTIVITY 3: Their Flaw

What inner weakness holds them back?

Circle one or write your own

Fear *Pride* *Guilt* *Envy* *Doubt*

Flaws make characters relatable. Let them stumble, but give them room to grow.

ACTIVITY 4: Their Circle

Who is one ally that helps them grow?

Who is one person who gets in their way (and maybe isn't evil)?

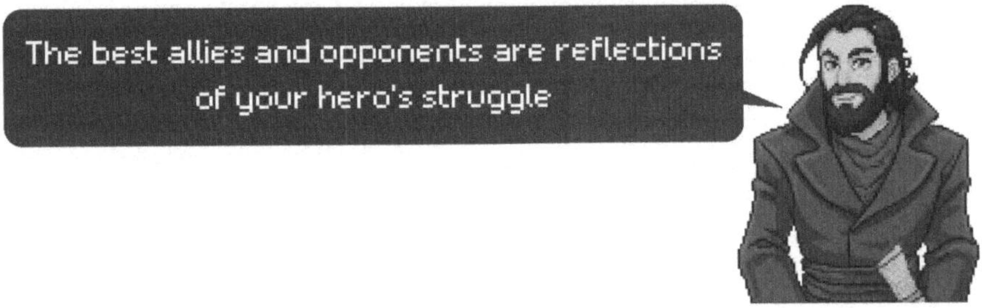

ACTIVITY 5: Inner Voice

Reflections!!!

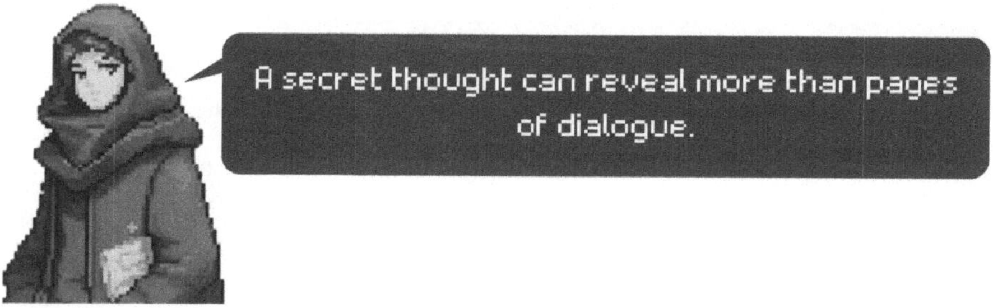

SPARK MOMENT

What event forces them to move? To change? To fight back?

Look for tension. A good spark always lights a fire.

Worldbuilder's Workshop

A world isn't just a place—it's a reflection.

Build a world your character needs, not just one that looks cool.

ACTIVITY 1: The Strange Rule

Invent one unusual rule or truth about this world. Something that hints at a deeper theme.

This strange detail can become the soul of your world.

ACTIVITY 2: What's Broken?

What's wrong in this world? What cries out for a story?

Think: What needs to be healed, uncovered, or overthrown?

ACTIVITY 3: The Culture

A strange custom or belief?
A powerful object people care about?
A symbol that means more than it seems?

Let culture breathe through tiny details. A festival. A rule. A piece of forbidden art.

ACTIVITY 4: Hidden Corners

Where does the world hide its secrets?

A cave, a ruin, a memory, a person?

Secrets are story seeds. Plant one and see what grows.

REFLECT: Link It Back

How does this world echo your character's flaw or need?

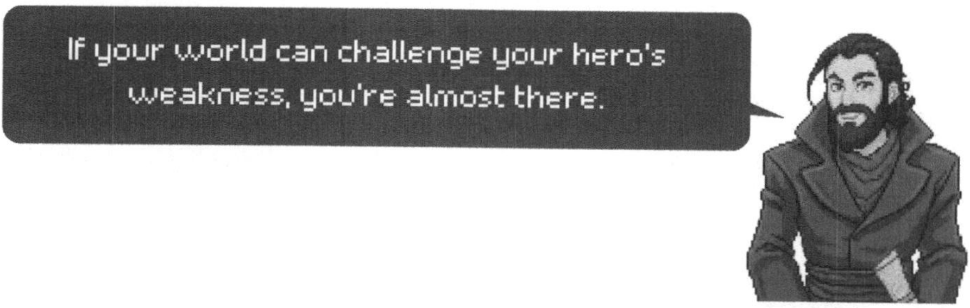

Plot Lab

<u>Where everything you've built starts to burn and breathe.</u>

A story isn't a line—it's a climb.

Let your character fall. Then show us how they rise.

STEP 1: The Spark

What unexpected moment changes everything?

The spark should raise a question the story must answer.

STEP 2: The Goal

What does your character want now more than ever?

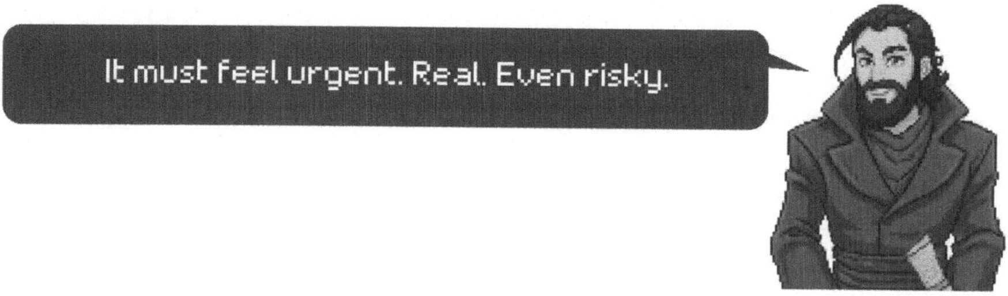

STEP 3: The Struggles

External (outside them)
Internal (inside them)

STEP 4: The Break

What gets shattered? A belief, a friendship, a rule?

STEP 5: The Clash

Describe the final confrontation.

This could be a fight, a speech, a choice—anything that costs something.

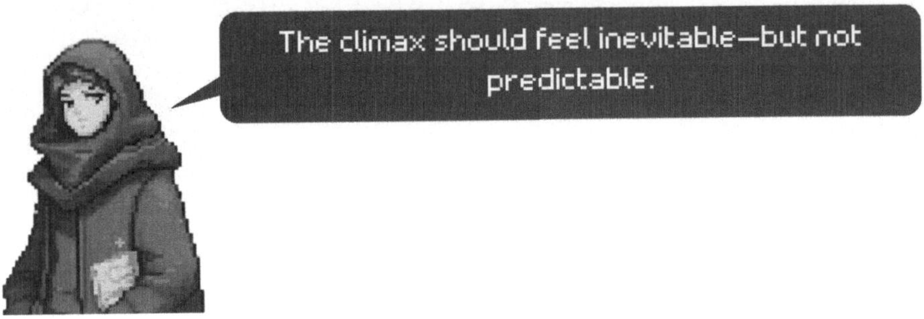

STEP 6: The Revelation

What truth do they finally see?

A truth about themselves or the world they never understood until now.

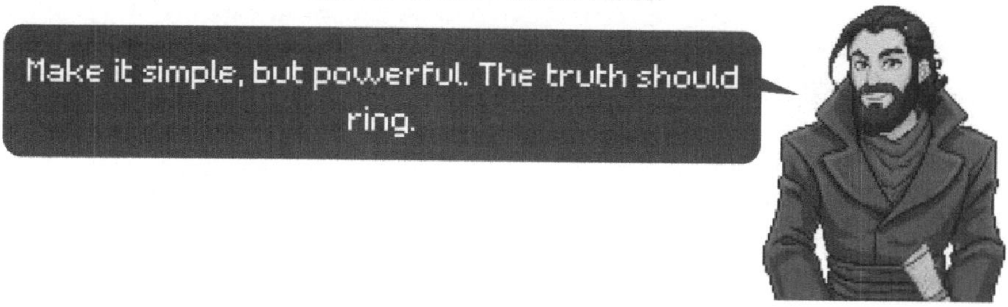

STEP 7: The New Ground

What does life look like after the storm?

It might be better, worse, or simply wiser.

The stories that shape the world begin when someone like you picks up a pen. Not to impress. Not to be perfect. Just to be brave.

BE PART OF THE UPCOMING EDITION

Your words matter. Your stories can move hearts, change minds, and light up corners of the world you've never seen.

Submit Your Story by Sending it to Us!

bladewoven@gmail.com

Must be your original work.

Selected entries will be featured in the next book!

INK MAY FADE, BUT YOUR STORY CAN OUTLIVE CENTURIES. IT ONLY BEGINS WHEN YOU DECIDE TO SHARE IT

This isn't the End. This is the beginning.

This is the Resurrection and the New Awakening.

9 789334 366860

Printed at Repro India Ltd.